My Down Syndrome Boy

Leila V. Nunes

DORRANCE PUBLISHING CO
EST. 1920
PITTSBURGH, PENNSYLVANIA 15238

Dorrance Publishing Co
585 Alpha Drive
Suite 103
Pittsburgh, PA 15238
Visit our website at *www.dorrancebookstore.com*

ISBN: 979-8-8860-4109-5
EISBN: 979-8-8860-4776-9

My Down Syndrome Boy

Every day, every night

He becomes more bright.

He always needs to be a guide

In this world we ride.

My boy and I

Always fly

Up above the sky

Not afraid of the high.

Along we go for a walk

Not worrying about how
much to talk.

We see beauty in our path

And pets taking a bath.

Do you understand, Sweetie?

On the way back home

We pretend that we see biome

We chatted about Down
Syndrome

And how fun is to get an extra
chromosome

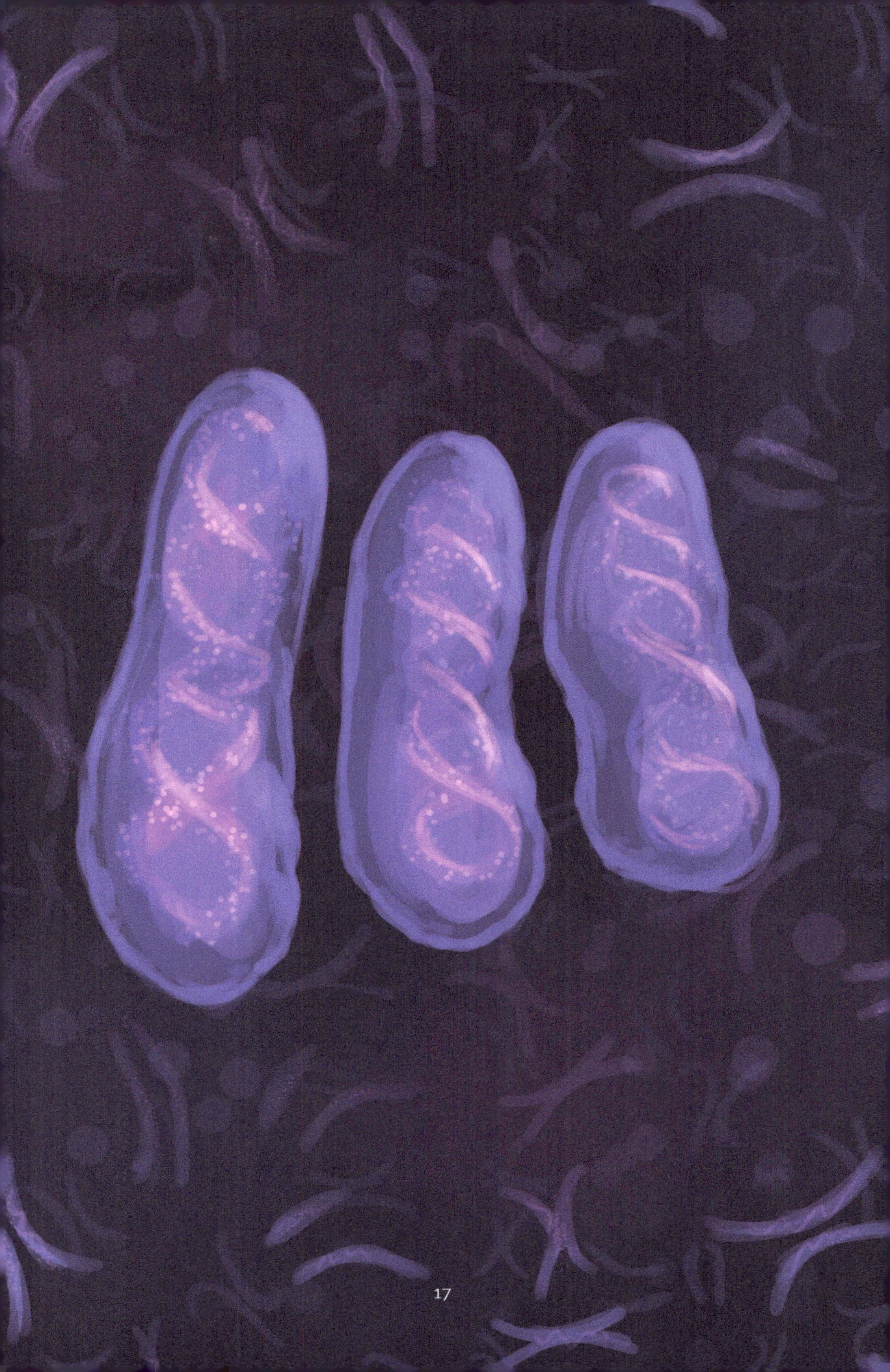

We love each other.

Why not? I am his mother

Who lives for his best

Until it's time to rest.